CONFESSIONS

of a Lukewarm

CHRISTIAN

CONFESSIONS

of a Lukewarm

CHRISTIAN

DICK BONT

ENDORSEMENTS

"Now we're Saved and Hungry! This book is so timely. My wife, Laurie, and I see so many parallels in *Confessions of a Lukewarm Christian* with our own journey over the past few years. What Dick describes seems like a common theme among a growing number of Christians today, whose eyes are opening to the truth that there is so much more available, so much more that God wants to share with us, if we realize what a relationship with Him can really be. People no longer go to church "because I'm supposed to," so they are waking up and asking, "Why am I?" (or "Why would I?"). Reading this helped shine a light on the path to "There's more!" and "What's next?" God is so much more than a safety net. Laurie and I didn't know what we didn't know. And now we are upset that no one told us sooner (and a little distressed that there are still so many in the dark—we hope that we can get our children to read this). This book *will* help others find a Spirit-led life. Thank you, Dick."

> — **Laurie and Mathew Crawford, friends of Dick and ministry partners**

"I, like Pastor Bont, was raised in a good Calvinistic church. I was baptized as an infant, made profession of faith in high school, and thought that was it. I was saved. But after reading Dick's book, I realize there is so much more to being a saved child of God. I recommend this book to anyone who is searching for a true biblical approach to living a real spirit-led Christian life. It will change your life!"

— Bob Goote, retired radio personality

"Dick Bont's passion is for every Christian to know and live the full, rich, joyous life of serving Jesus, the King of Kings and Lord of Lords, so that His Great Love will overflow into a lost and hurting world. Dick's journey recounted in this book is one that will help others toward an authentic relationship with the Living God."

— Rev. Mike Gatliff, nursing home chaplain

ISBN: 978-0-578-61450-2

Cover design by Cooper Alan
Page layout by Win-Win Words LLC

Printed in the United States of America

CONTENTS

FOREWORD

Pastor Dick Bont's new book, *Confessions of a
Lukewarm Christian*, is his most timely and important literary work thus far. While *Life As It Should
Be* is an insightful, thought-provoking, game-changer
of a project (as are his other works), *Confessions of a
Lukewarm Christian* really should be read first to
clearly understand where we, as "believers," presently
stand in our relationship with Jesus.

Pastor Dick's transparent, easy-to-read, person-
able style of writing will invariably cause one to desire to investigate their own motives set against
Biblical truths in regard to their journey with Christ
from sanctification to salvation—and on to the po-
tential rewards that await Christians in heaven.

I encourage all to let this powerful book be your
roadmap to spiritual discovery and motive.

Of course, no one can put a prompt on the table
like the Word of God itself as found in the Bible. To
that end, please read what Jesus Himself tells us concerning on-the-fence Christians: *Revelation 3:16*:

"So, because you are lukewarm—neither hot nor cold—I am about to spit you out of my mouth." (NIV)

And how about another scripture penned by Paul as inspired by the Holy Spirit in *1 Corinthians 3:12-15*, which makes it expressly clear how important the subject of our position in Christ really is to God: "Now if anyone builds on the foundation with gold, silver, precious stones, wood, hay, straw, each one's work will become manifest, for the Day will disclose it, because it will be revealed by fire, and the fire will test what sort of work each one has done. If the work that anyone has built on the foundation survives, he will receive a reward. If anyone's work is burned up, he will suffer loss, though he himself will be saved, but only as through fire."(NIV)

At such a time as this, each of us surely should personally assess our standing in Christ Jesus: Do we really want to get into heaven by the "skin of our teeth"? Will we be culled-out by God's refining fire only to find we were never really saved? My point is, if there is a sense at the epicenter of your heart and spirit that longs to clarify whether there is more to knowing Jesus than just being saved, it's beyond worth investigating! And in doing so, perhaps you might realize a calling, or a higher purpose for your existence? I believe *now* is the time to review our priorities and get *all in* with God's redemptive plan.

The Bible tells us that we exist to learn more about God's Word and character, to be empowered and gifted by the Holy Spirit, and to witness as Ambassadors of The Gospel of Grace throughout the world in Jesus's name for the Glory of God.

My prayer for all of us is not just to be "saved and satisfied." If we are, it will not only be our loss, but a loss to others as well.

Each of us is a unique, individual part of the Body of Christ—His Bride: Jesus is waiting for us to choose Him above all else. What an honor. And to that end, what a great book you're about to read!

Grace and peace,
Jennifer O'Neill
Founder of Jennifer O'Neill Ministries, Inc.,
    model, actress, speaker, and author
www.jenniferoneill.com

ACKNOWLEDGMENTS

F IRST OF ALL, I WANT to thank God for His patience and grace toward me, which allowed the journey described in this book to take place.

Second, I want to thank my wife, Beth, and our family for their continued love and support.

Third, as with my other books, I want to thank my friend and sister in Christ, Jen. Without her help, advice, and support, this book would not have happened.

Finally, continued thanks to all my ministry partners and friends whose love, support, and encouragement keep me writing.

INTRODUCTION

What does it mean to be lukewarm, or as it is also called, "saved and satisfied"?

L ET'S START WITH ME, KNOWING that there are many more people out there who struggle with this condition. We are those who are happy with where we are in our Christian life. We are saved by the blood of Jesus into eternal life; at least we hope so. Because of that, we don't have to worry about hell, but sometimes we do. How about you? Do you function on the outside like you are fine spiritually, but inside you sense something isn't quite right? Have you settled into a routine of being a Christian, but often the thrill is gone? What does that mean? Let's talk.

I have been there. I am writing this book to you and to me. I have discovered five areas of my life in which I had deceived myself into thinking that I was happy being ignorant. There are five areas that, by the grace of God, through which I have come to a new understanding. I have come to realize that God wants an intimate, personal, ongoing, growing relationship with me. That's why Jesus died for me, not just to save me, but also to bring me into that relationship with God. He gave me the Holy Spirit to lead, guide, and empower me in that relationship. I have come to know that regardless of what any earthly father is like, God as my heavenly Father is perfect. I was blessed with a good, godly, earthly father who loved me. But my heavenly Father is infinitely better than my dad ever could be. For those reading this book who had a negative, unloving, cruel, earthly father, God is infinitely more than the loving father you longed to have. He is loving, gracious, forgiving, and kind beyond your comprehension, and He wants to have a loving relationship with His children. Now I know what I was missing by just being saved and satisfied. I am here on this earth for God's glory and purposes, and that far exceeded my wildest imaginations!

I invite you to come along with me on my journey of discovery. I pray that when you do, through the power and the anointing of the Holy Spirit, this book will lead you into the life that God has planned specifically for you.

CONFESSIONS

of a Lukewarm

CHRISTIAN

I

SAVED AND SATISFIED

I REALLY BELIEVED THAT I was OK. I was saved, and I figured that was all that mattered. When you are born into a church-going Christian family, it is hard, because of your heritage, to not feel saved. If that family is fairly legalistic, you grow up striving to do all the right things, according to the dictates of your traditions. I learned early on that if I did all this well, I would meet with my parents' approval, get noticed by church leadership, and, most importantly, I thought God would be pleased with me and continue to love me.

I soon discovered I had been mistaken. That's when I learned that God's love and my behavior were in a *cause-and-effect relationship*. I remember my mother saying things such as, "If you don't dress in your very best clothes to go to church, you must not love God, and He will not be pleased with you." I had this performance-based relationship with God, without realizing at the time that while I believed He judged me on my performance, I was also judging

Him on His. *When you are in a performance state of mind, it flows both ways.*

As a result of this tenuous relationship, my questioning of God's love for me became a regular thing. How could He love me when I continued to perform so poorly? And how could I trust Him when He did things that I couldn't understand? So, I spent a lot of time traveling to places like *Guilt City* and *Shame Island.* The idea of giving myself completely to God, which is what I was told I was supposed to do, was risky at best. To my way of thinking, if I went all in with God, I would have to be super good and give up a lot. That first part I knew I couldn't do, and I didn't know if I wanted to do the second.

I didn't know at that time that giving it all to God had little to do with my behavior and everything to do with the condition of my heart. God needed my heart right so He could do everything in and through my life that He wanted to do. *I was beginning to learn that every aspect of my life had much more to do with who God was than who I was.* But, I still had a long way to go in learning that.

My family didn't talk much about grace; we were too busy trying to abide by all the rules! The only grace that I knew was a cat so named owned by my friend who lived down the street. Up to this stage in my life, and for a long while after, I missed out on the amazing all-encompassing grace of God. Without grace, all I had left was my own effort, so I tried my best to do all the steps well, and I was pretty successful at it.

I was considered a good Christian young adult. I followed the rules, didn't do too much wrong (that anyone was aware of), and was definitely saved as far as anyone could tell. When you are told something enough times, you tend to believe it. I was told often enough that I was saved that I believed that it must be true. That made me feel good because it removed my excessive fear of going to hell. If heaven and hell were real, and I believed they were, I figured early on which one I wanted to go to. As a result, I became *saved and satisfied*. I could now live my life knowing that I had reached my spiritual goal. As an added bonus, I had made my parents happy.

A quick word about my parents: They both dearly loved the Lord and were absolutely sincere in what they did. Some of the ways in which they expressed their love for Him were by going to church, having devotions, helping those in need, and having strict rules for Sunday observance. But there was also a lot of obligation, performance, and legalism in what they did. Don't get me wrong, I am extremely thankful for my heritage, but there were some things that messed me up a little. In no way do I blame my parents; it is all on me. One of the things that I wish I could have changed is that my father passed away before I went into the ministry at age forty-six. I think he would have been proud of my decision; I know that my mom was.

As I transitioned into my twenties, a lot of things changed. I got married, started having kids, and found a job I liked. One thing that didn't change, however, was my *saved and satisfied life.* I continued to perform well. I had morning devotions (sometimes); I faithfully took my family to church; and I prayed and read the Bible at meals. . . . These were all the things that I had been taught that good Christians do. My family was looked at as one of the "good ones" in the church. Of course, no one knew what was really going on.

My marriage was in trouble, and all my 'performing' couldn't fix it. After my marriage eventually failed, my *saved and satisfied* life fell apart. It was even more confusing for me because, a number of years earlier, on my own volition, I had sincerely asked Jesus to come into my heart as my Savior. I was in a hotel in Indiana on a business trip, and I was struck by the fact that I had never really asked Jesus into my heart. So, I got down on my knees and prayed, "Jesus, I know that I am a sinner and that my sin is keeping me from You. I know that you died on the cross so my sins would be forgiven. Please forgive my sins and come into my heart and be my Savior. Amen."

Later in life I realized that I had missed some things in that prayer (mainly the part about asking Jesus to also be the Lord of my life), but at the time it seemed like I had covered everything. So why were my marriage, my life, and my world falling apart?

Maybe I wasn't as close to God as I thought? I did recover with help from a good counselor and some friends. Even though I still wasn't where I should have been with Him, I knew that God was my main help. But, soon after recovery, I went back to my *saved and satisfied* ways.

I heard what the minister preached on Sunday, but it was hard to really listen—after all, I had some important things to think about; my mind wandered a lot. Besides, there were a number of things that made me feel confused and uncomfortable. Things like the following:

• *Baptism.* I was confused as to what I had been taught as opposed to what I later learned about what the Bible said. I had been baptized as an infant and was told that was good enough. I was taught that baptism was the sign that you were part of God's covenant family. Something about that was very cool. The whole congregation would commit to cover you with prayer and support until you reached the wondrous age of understanding: the time when you were old enough to understand what you were doing and what it meant. That magical age in the denomination in which I grew up was somewhere in your middle-teenage years—fourteen to sixteen years old.

Here's how it was supposed to work: In arguably the most confusing season of your life, you are told to make the most important decision of your life. When the time came that you were "ready" (often determined by how many of your friends were ready, too), you went before the elders of the church. Then they asked you some questions. If the answers were satisfactory, you would go before the congregation and make your public profession of faith. . . . At that point your journey to salvation was complete. What was interesting to me, is that you were never asked to actually give a testimony. You simply answered a few questions about whether you were willing to receive Christ and commit to Him, but you never had to say the words of true repentance and commitment. You just had to answer "Yes."

Maybe that is where the 'saved and satisfied gene' first got planted in me.

Anyway, that is how it was done in the denomination in which I grew up in. But I knew that the Bible said you had to *believe first* and *then* be baptized, based on your own decision.

I had been a pretty intelligent kid, but not smart enough to make a commitment like that at eight weeks old. On the other hand, I had no interest in standing in front of the whole congregation in some oversized robe while the pastor dunked me in some water. I don't even like water.

• *The Ten Commandments.* Now there's an impossible list of rules to follow. Did God really expect me to do all that? What if I messed up—which I was pretty sure I would do frequently?

• *The Sermon on the Mount.* This was beyond impossible. How could anybody live this kind of life?

This went much deeper than my actions. According to this set of teachings by Jesus, my thoughts and motives also had to be perfect. There was just no way I could do that.

• *The Great Commission.* Talk about frightening. I went out and bought a new shovel because I didn't dare confront my neighbor about getting back the one he borrowed from me: How am I supposed to talk to complete strangers about something I don't even fully understand myself? What if I get rejected? I was a salesman, and a good one, so I wasn't rejected often, but I hated it when I was. Setting myself up for failure didn't make a lot of sense.

• *Holy Spirit.* This was so confusing to me. I knew that I had received it when I was saved, but what did that mean and who was "it"? I heard talk, but not very often, about filling and refilling of the Holy Spirit, about being baptized with and/or into the Holy Spirit, about receiving and giving myself to His leadings. . . . It all made my head swim. It was as if the Holy Spirit were the *red-headed stepchild of the Trinity* who was only talked about in hushed tones on certain occasions. Then, at other times, He was the key to living the life God wanted me to live.

The same confusion was there when I read the Bible for devotions; which I did fairly regularly. So, I missed a lot; passages like:

1. In *Deuteronomy 6:5* we are commanded to, "Love the Lord your God with all your heart, with all your soul, and with all your strength."

2. *I Corinthians 6:19* reminds us, "Do you not know that your body is a temple of the Holy Spirit, who is in you, whom you received from God? You are not your own; you were bought at a price."

3. In *Romans 12:1*, the Apostle Paul urges us, "in view of God's mercy, to offer your bodies as living sacrifices, holy and pleasing to God—which is your spiritual act of worship."

4. *Galatians 2:20* makes it clear when Paul says, "I have been crucified with Christ and I no longer live, but Christ lives in me. The life I live in the body, I live by faith in the Son of God, who loved me and gave Himself for me."

5. In *John 14:21*, Jesus, Himself, tells us, "Whoever has my commands and obeys them, he is the one who loves me. He who loves me will be loved by my Father, and I too will love him and show myself to him."

I also must have missed all that the Bible says about the things that I could fully experience if I gave myself completely to God and allowed the Holy Spirit not only to lead me—*but also to empower me*. Amazing things like:

1. LOVE: *I John 3:1* – "How great is the love that the Father has lavished on us that we should be called children of God."

2. FORGIVENESS: *Colossians 2:13-14* – "When you were dead in your sins and in the uncircumcision of your sinful nature, God made you alive with Christ. He forgave us all our sins . . . "

3. POWER: *Acts 1:8* – "But you will receive power when the Holy Spirit comes on you . . . "

4. FREEDOM: *Galatians 5:13* – You, my brothers, were called to be free. But do not use your freedom to indulge your sinful nature, rather, serve one another in love."

5. PEACE: *John 14:27* – "Peace I leave with you; My peace I give you. I do not give to you as the world gives. Do not let your hearts be troubled, and do not be afraid."

6. ABUNDANT LIFE: *John 10:10* – " . . . I have come that you may have life, and have it to the full."

7. PRESENCE: *John 14:20* – "On that day (When the Holy Spirit comes) you will realize that I am in My Father, and you are in Me, and I am in you."

I have to admit that there were a few passages that scared me a little . . . OK, *a lot*. They were the ones that talked about being lukewarm, like *Revelation 3:15-17*: "I know your deeds, that you are neither cold nor hot. I wish you were either one or the other! So, because you are lukewarm—neither hot nor cold—I am about to spit you out of my mouth. You say, 'I am rich; I have acquired wealth and do not need a thing.' But you do not realize that you are wretched, pitiful, poor, blind, and naked."

I had heard enough about the Holy Spirit to know that if anyone truly accepted Jesus as Lord and Savior, they received the Holy Spirit. I also heard that the Holy Spirit did amazing things in believers' lives. One of those things was to prompt us to want to give more of ourselves to God. If I had no desire, then maybe I had quenched the Holy Spirit, and *I Thessalonians 5:19* commands us: "Do not quench the Spirit's fire."

Or even worse, I never had the Holy Spirit in the first place, which would possibly make *Matthew 7:21-23* apply to me: "Not everyone who says to me, 'Lord, Lord,' will enter the kingdom of heaven, but only the one who does the will of my Father who is in heaven. Many will say to me on that day, 'Lord, Lord, did we not prophesy in your name and in your name drive out demons and, in your name, perform many miracles?

"Then I will tell them plainly, 'I never knew you. Away from Me, you evildoers!'"

When my minister started talking about those kinds of things, I did whatever I could to shut him out. I believed that I was saved, most of the time, but there were also times of doubt and a lot of not caring. So, while on the one hand I thought I was OK, on the other I had this nagging thought that maybe I wasn't as saved as I thought. . . . *Can I be half-saved?*

I convinced myself that we are all on a spiritual journey, and every one of us is at a different place on that journey. I also accepted that the issue was not so much where I was on the journey, *but where my heart was*—and my heart was fine right where it was, or so I thought.

In short, while I claimed to be a Christian:

1. I still set my own boundaries.
2. I still operated under the world's system.
3. I still tried to get my needs met in my own way.
4. I still let the world set my standards.
5. I didn't really want God; I wanted what I could get from Him.
6. I thought of God the way I would think of another person, only He was much more demanding and powerful, so at times I tried a little harder.
7. I had given God my life, but only the parts I didn't really want to hang onto.

My attitude was:

"You died for me; thank you, Jesus. Now you want me to do what? I don't think so. I will show that I love you by performing the way I think you want me to—but within my own boundaries and limitations."

Still, despite myself, I was beginning to feel some deeper movement toward God. The Holy Spirit was nudging me closer. I was beginning to recognize that He was my guide and source of truth, and that God was not about to leave me alone. I began to believe that maybe God did love me. I had never questioned His love for anybody else, only for me. I was starting to see how prideful that was. . . .

Although it didn't move me very far out of my *saved and satisfied* thinking, it was a start.

Moving Toward Growth:

1. How has your upbringing affected your spiritual journey?

2. Is there ever a time in your walk with God that you can say, "I have grown enough. I am content where I am"?

3. Are there any verses in the Bible that make you feel uncomfortable when you hear them? Why?

4. What has kept you from giving yourself completely to God?

5. Would you call yourself *saved and satisfied*? Why or why not?

2

MY
SELF-DECEPTION
ABOUT 'SELF'

**If what I want is more important to me than what
God wants for me, who am I really serving?**

Joshua 22:5:
"But be very careful to keep the commandment and
the law that Moses the servant of the Lord gave
you: to love the Lord your God, to walk in obedience to Him, to keep His commands, to hold fast
to Him and to serve Him with all your heart and
with all your soul."

I REMEMBER HEARING AN ILLUSTRATION that used marriage as an example. It went something like this:
A boy meets a girl, they fall in love, and boy and
girl get married. So far, so good. Once the wedding
and honeymoon are over, the husband sits his wife
down and says to her, "I want you to know that my
goal was only to get married. Don't expect anything
from me. I am not interested in growing together
with you or improving our relationship. I only want

to do what feels good to me, so don't ask me to give more to this marriage than I want to. I do expect, however, that you will be available when I want you to be or need you to be. I appreciate what you did to make this marriage possible. Just don't ask more from me because I am totally satisfied with how things are right now."

That might sound a little extreme. Let's try this theme: The husband tells his wife, "I love you and I am committed to you, but you need to know that there are some things that I am not going to give up for you. I want to continue to go out with my buddies a few times a month; I want a certain amount of time to myself; and don't even think about asking me to give up deer hunting."

It didn't take me much time to realize that at different stages of my life I had been the husband in both scenarios. No, I didn't speak either of those proclamations or ultimatums to my wife. I was too good a husband to do something like that. But in essence, I had said those things to God.

My life was moving along quite nicely. I had struggled with many of the same things that most kids in their late teens struggle with: identity, school, future plans, and, of course, girls. Spiritually, I thought that I had it all together. I knew more about the Bible than most kids my age. I could hold my own in most religious discussions; in fact, if I am honest, I was kind of a know-it-all. I was humble on the outside, but pride was running rampant inside me. My knowledge, instead of drawing me closer to God, actually allowed my *saved and satisfied* life to flourish because what I knew was only head knowledge, and that was good enough for me. I was a living example of *Isaiah 29:13,* where it says: "These people come near to Me with their mouth, and honor Me with their lips, but their hearts are far from Me. Their worship of Me is made up only of rules taught by men."

Something in me was beginning to stir. I knew at eighteen years old that I was going to be in the ministry someday. It wasn't a plan or ambition; it was just something I knew was going to happen. I didn't think about it a lot because it wasn't something that drove me. However, every once in a while, it would hit me that I had this "vision" inside me, although it made no sense to me because I was not the kind of guy who was "ministry material." I think that touch on my heart was the beginning of my journey that eventually led me out of my *saved and satisfied* life. I say journey because it took me twenty-eight years to get there. It's something that I attribute to the fact that, spiritually, I am a really slow learner. The truth is, I liked my life. Even though I knew what was required to live a more godly life, I wasn't ready to make the changes necessary to get there. Or, if I'm honest, I really didn't want to. My life, my way, was still more important to me than what God wanted.

I recall one time when I was in church listening to the minister preach on something that Asaph had written concerning the place of God in his life in *Psalms 73:25,* where it says:

"Whom have I in heaven but You? And earth has nothing I desire besides You."

I remember thinking at the time that I understood the first part of the verse (I found out later that I didn't get it as well as I thought), but the second part wasn't true for me. I didn't care about what I might be missing; I only thought about what I might have to give up. For instance, there was the issue of an addiction I was dealing with, that on the one hand caused me to feel great guilt, and on the other hand, I didn't want to let go of it. I wasn't quite sure how God would react to that, so I deemed it better to keep it to myself (which was beyond foolish of me, since I knew that God knows everything).

One of the things I was beginning to realize is that I didn't know as much about grace as I thought I did. I didn't realize for instance that:

- God's grace was far greater than my sin.
- God's grace was flowing into my life constantly, if I allowed it to.
- The recognition of my constant need for God's grace is what kept me dependent on Him.
- God's grace and God's love go hand in hand.
- God's grace, through the Holy Spirit, empowered me to be victorious over sin.

I was starting to realize that the more that I

learned on this journey, the less I actually knew. I still had a long way to go.

I was also beginning to realize that being *saved and satisfied* didn't bring me closer to God . . . it kept me away from Him. It was just my way of keeping God at arm's length so I could continue to live the life that I wanted to live. I was using my salvation as a license, not to do bad things but to live my life my way. I was a pretender. I was doing all the right religious things, calling myself a Christ follower, but having no real relationship with Him. I began to feel like a fraud, and I think I know why.

During one of the few times I was actually listening in church, I remember hearing about the Holy Spirit. It's not like I had never heard of Him before (remember the red-headed stepchild), but for some reason this time I paid attention to what was being taught.

The minister was talking about Pentecost and the sermon that Peter preached to the people in *Acts 2* and especially what was said at the end of the sermon in *verse 38:*

"Peter replied, 'Repent and be baptized, every one of you, in the Name of Jesus Christ for the forgiveness of your sins. And you will receive the gift of the Holy Spirit.'"

I realized for the first time that I had received more than salvation when I was saved; I had also received the Holy Spirit.

To be honest, I really had no idea what that

meant, but I wanted to find out. So I began to really read and study my Bible in order to discover what being saved actually meant. Most of what I learned about were things that I had heard many times before, but they had never sunk in. But now, through the wisdom of the Holy Spirit, things were starting to make sense.

For now, I want to share the truths that I was beginning to learn about myself, because that is where I find myself in my confession.

Probably the hardest thing to admit about myself is that I was guilty of idolatry, and that was keeping me from learning the truth. I heard someone once say :

"God is God, but He does not become my God until I obey Him. Whatever I obey is my god."

But in reality, I was obeying me. Jesus told His disciples in *John 14:23*:

" . . . If anyone loves Me, he will obey My teaching."

Jesus summarized His teaching in *Matthew 22:37* when He said:

"Love the Lord your God with all your heart and with all your soul and with all your mind. This is the first and greatest commandment."

I came to realize that *anything* can be an idol. Whatever I place above God in my life is an idol. In *Isaiah 44* God makes His feelings toward idolatry very evident, and in *verse 6*, in His own words, He makes it clear who He is:

"This is what the Lord says—Israel's King and Redeemer, the Lord Almighty: I am the first and I am the last; *apart from Me there is no God.*"

I was finally beginning to accept that loving God above all, and giving myself completely to Him, was a command—not a request.

I was also beginning to see that being a Christ follower meant so much more than just being saved. It was also starting to sink in for me that salvation had much more to do with who *God* is rather than who *I* am.

I was starting to feel that I just might be missing out on something—something really big, and I considered the possibility that the Holy Spirit was prompting that feeling in me. Still, I just wasn't sure.

So, I continued my *saved and satisfied* ways, but with less surety.

Moving Toward Growth:

1. Discuss the question at the beginning of this chapter. If what I want is more important to me than what God wants for me, who am I really serving?

2. Define grace, and describe how it functions in your life.

3. Talk about the quote, "God is God, but He does not become my God until I obey Him. Whatever I obey is my god."

4. What things in your life could be considered idols (more important to you than God)?

3
MY SELF-DECEPTION ABOUT SATISFACTION

Am I really so satisfied by what the world has to offer that I don't want what God has *already given*?

Isaiah 55:2:
"Why spend money on what is not bread, and your labor on what does not satisfy? Listen, listen to Me, and eat what is good, and your soul will delight in the richest of fare."

I ALWAYS LOOKED AT THE search for satisfaction and contentment as a normal pursuit. In fact, everybody seemed to be trying to find a life that they could be happy with as if they were born with a desire to find something that would reward them. So I joined the masses of people looking for the missing piece that would bring happiness and satisfaction to my life. I figured that I had a step up on everyone else because I prayed and asked God to help me, never realizing that *He* was the missing piece. It seemed like that was what God would want for me. Right?

Still, even with God's "help," I admit that things were not always easy. When my first wife and I got married, we didn't have much. It was a struggle to pay the bills. We never went on vacations; we hardly ever went out just to eat. Then we started having kids, and while they brought great joy, they also made things more difficult, especially in the area of finances. But we got by.

Things started getting better when I rediscovered my niche: sales. I had always been able to speak well and present information in a logical and understandable way, so sales was a natural fit, and I was very good at it. It didn't matter what it was, I could sell it. As someone once said, "He could sell cat food to dogs." So, even though I had to spend a lot of time away from my family, I became somewhat successful. As a good humble Christian, I attributed my gains to God's helping me. The truth was, other than an occasional prayer and attending church when I could make it, I didn't think about God that much. I did have these nagging questions in the back of my mind, though: "What if God took it all away? Where would I find my satisfaction then?"

As I was coasting along in my life, God did an amazing thing. He brought a spiritual mentor into my life. He was one of my wife's former teachers, a family friend, and the most spiritual man I knew. What amazed me most about our mentoring relationship was how it came about.

We used to take walks together so we could talk, mostly about spiritual things. On one of our little tours around the block, he said, "I decided that I need an accountability partner. I am struggling with some things, and I need someone that I can trust to hold me accountable. Would you be that person?" I was floored. Here was this spiritual giant (in my estimation) asking me, a *saved and satisfied* spiritual weakling (by comparison) to be his accountability partner. I reluctantly agreed, and that started a deeper relationship. It became one of the things that God used to show that He had much more to offer me than the *saved and satisfied* life I was living.

Everyone has their own thing in which they find satisfaction; mine was family. My family was not perfect; in fact, it would later fall apart through divorce, but at this point in my life, my family was more than enough. I was in my late twenties, had three great kids, and my marriage was good, I thought. In short, I was a blessed man. In fact, one of the big reasons I was reluctant to give my life completely to God was because I thought He might take someone in my family away. I remembered the story in the Bible, in *Genesis 22:2*, in which God told Abraham:

"Take your son, your only son, Isaac, whom you love, and go to the region of Moriah. Sacrifice him there as a burnt offering on one of the mountains I will tell you about."

I found out later that God's demand was just a test and Abraham passed. I'm not so sure that I would have. The best way to prevent that from happening to my kids was to hang on to them by my own strength. But those same questions kept coming up: "What if I did lose someone? Would I ever find satisfaction again? *Worst, would God test me like He did Abraham?*"

I was beginning to recognize two very important things about myself: first, I was pursuing the same things in the same way everyone else was (even those who were not Christians). So my life wasn't really any different than anyone else's. Second, the things that I was seeking in order to find satisfaction, contentment, and happiness were fleeting, at best. Life is short, after all. I guess the words of *I John 2:15-17* were finally starting to sink in:

"Do not love the world or anything in the world. If anyone loves the world, love for the Father is not in them. For everything in the world—the lust of the flesh, the lust of the eyes, and the pride of life—comes not from the Father but from the world. The world and its desires pass away, but whoever does the will of God lives forever."

I was trying to have it both ways. While watching a television program the other day, I heard a great illustration of this notion. One of the characters in the show was coming down the stairs, and one of the other characters asked, "How are you?" Her answer was classic: She replied, "I'm right with my Savior and tight with my bookie." WOW! Talk about wanting one foot in the world and one in the kingdom. But I was just as bad—I wanted everything the world had to offer, and I wanted God's blessing, too. I hadn't paid attention when the Bible says very clearly in places like *James 4:4*:

"You, adulterous people, don't you know that friendship with the world is hatred toward God? Anyone who chooses to be a friend of the world becomes an enemy of God."

It was becoming abundantly clear to me that I had been on the rocky side of my path. It was not so much that what I was pursuing was wrong, it was the *why* that made all the difference. If I had honestly been *seeking* God and His plan for my life, trusting Him to give me only what He wanted me to have through His grace, the rest of the stuff would be all right. I was doing just the opposite—*as my satisfaction level increased, my need for God decreased.* Again, if I am honest, I was trying to fit into a world that, as a Christian, I should not want to fit into. After all, the world is a system that tries to exist without the one true God, Who is revealed in the Bible. While the concept of "being in the world, but not of the world" was still confusing me, I was becoming aware that I was way too much "of the world." Something had to change.

As my journey continued, I discovered that my thinking and my desires were beginning to change. I was no longer satisfied with the life I was living. I was remembering things from the Bible that I didn't even know were in my head. The work of the Holy

Spirit was becoming evident in my life. Rather than scaring me as it once did, I welcomed Him. In fact, He was someone I *needed* if I was going to become more of *who God wanted me to be*.

But I still had a couple of major hurdles that I had to deal with.

Moving Toward Growth:

1. Discuss the question at the beginning of the chapter: Am I really so satisfied by what the world has to offer that I don't want what God has *already given*?

2. How would you handle life if you lost everything that was important to you?

3. If someone observed your life for a period of time, what would they say is more important to you: your relationship with the world or your relationship with God?

4. *Matthew 6:33* says, "Seek first the Kingdom of God and His righteousness, and all these things (the needs of life) will be given to you as well." What would change in your life if you really lived this verse?

4
MY
SELF-DECEPTION
ABOUT GOODNESS

**If whatever human goodness I might have had
wasn't good enough to save me, why would
I think it might be good enough now
to bring me closer to God?**

Colossians 2:6-7:
"So then, just as you received Christ Jesus as Lord,
continue to live your lives in Him, rooted and built
up in Him, strengthened in the faith as you were
taught, and overflowing with thankfulness."

M Y POINT IS THAT I had a lot of friends, was
generally liked by most everybody, and
didn't have any real enemies . . . so my *goodness* had
served me well. *Kind of sounds like a good Boy
Scout, doesn't it?*

But my self-described goodness was also my
problem: First, because it wasn't always based on
honesty. I was a *people pleaser*, so sometimes my
kindness toward others was motivated by a need to

be liked rather than a pure heart. I didn't understand yet that, to God, *our motives are more important than our behavior.* God not only wants us to do the right thing, He wants us to do the right thing for the right reason. *Hebrews 4:12-13* tells us:

"For the word of God is living and active. Sharper than any double-edged sword, it penetrates even to dividing soul and spirit, joints and marrow; it judges the thoughts and attitudes of the heart. Nothing in all creation is hidden from God's sight. Everything is uncovered and laid bare before the eyes of Him to whom we must give account."

The second problem in regard to my so-called goodness was even bigger: It was keeping me from really appreciating what God had done when He sent Jesus to die on the cross for me. It was also keeping me from recognizing my ever-increasing need for the Holy Spirit to lead, guide, and strengthen me on a moment-by-moment basis. I should have realized that if I thought I could live my life every day on my own strength without ever thinking about God, I was sorely mistaken and misguided.

The Bible tells us in *Luke 7:44-47* the story of the woman who anointed Jesus's feet at the home of Simon. As the woman was anointing His feet, Jesus turned to Simon and said:

"Do you see this woman? I came into your house. You did not give Me any water for My feet, but she wet My feet with her tears and wiped them with her hair. You did not give Me a kiss, but this woman, from the time I entered, has not stopped kissing My feet. You did not put oil on My head, but she has poured perfume on My feet.

"Therefore, I tell you, her many sins have been forgiven—as her great love has shown. But whoever has been forgiven little loves little."

I was letting my so-called goodness come between me and the indescribable gift of salvation. *I had lost sight of the fact that no greater sacrifice has ever been given, no greater love has ever been shown, and no other act in human history deserved my gratitude more.* I needed to remember that, when it comes to salvation in Christ Jesus, no one has been "forgiven little."

I failed to note that good things done in my own strength, that come out of my own needs and desires, *did not impress God.* Nor did all my religiosity like going to church, tithing, devotions, etc. that were prompted by my need to try and please God— to impress Him. According to His Word in *Isaiah 66:2*, God tells us what impresses Him when He says:

"This is the one I esteem: he who is humble and contrite in spirit, and trembles at My Word."

God is not impressed with our self-prompted acts of goodness. He is impressed when we, in love, humility, gratitude, and obedience, give ourselves to Him and others to be used for *His glory.*

The necessity of giving myself completely to God to be used for His glory was becoming more and more clear. Also, the idea of going into the ministry that He had put into my heart years before was changing from just an idea into a real desire. *While I was beginning to understand the command to be "all in" with God, I continued to struggle with what that meant for my life in a practical sense.*

Did "giving myself" completely to God mean that I could never go on vacation, play golf, or simply have fun? Did it mean that I had to spend 24/7 witnessing to others and helping the poor?

While I was intent on trying to find the balance between living completely for God and enjoying the blessings He had given me, I still concluded that, for the time being, I was fine where I was. I was enjoying my fun-satisfied life. After all, I told myself, no one could really give themselves *completely* to God. Was it even possible to forget about yourself entirely and do only what God commanded you to do? Besides, I knew that I was going to heaven, so I didn't see a problem. Needless to say, I had missed something very crucial: the fact that God had equipped me with the Holy Spirit to be able to discern His will for my life, *if my heart was right and if I would slow down enough to listen.* You see, the Holy Spirit whispers; He doesn't shout over the noise of life. If I was going to hear Him, I would have to stop rushing and start really hearing. He had also given me guidelines in His Word to help direct me to the balanced life He wanted for me (not that I always obeyed them), but one in particular stuck out:

I Corinthians 10:31:

"So, whether you eat or drink or whatever you do, do it all for the glory of God."

Another one is found in *Galatians 5:13*:

"You, my brothers, were called to be free. Do not use your freedom to indulge your sinful nature; rather serve one another in love."

My next self-deception ended up being the biggest piece of the puzzle that finally put it all together for me—albeit, seemingly in slow motion.

Moving Toward Growth:

1. Discuss the question at the beginning of the chapter: If whatever human goodness I might have had wasn't good enough to save me, why would I think it might be good enough now to bring me closer to God?

2. In what ways do you try to impress God with your goodness?

3. Is there anything you can do to impress God? If so, what is it?

4. Do you ever struggle with the balance between living your life completely for God and enjoying the blessings He has given you?

5

MY
SELF-DECEPTION
ABOUT BEING SAVED

**Is being saved God's only goal for me,
or is there something more that I am missing?**

II Corinthians 5:20-21:
"We are therefore Christ's ambassadors, as though
God were making His appeal through us. We implore
you on Christ's behalf: Be reconciled to God. God
made Him who had no sin to be sin for us, so that in
Him we might become the righteousness of God."

T HERE IS SO MUCH HERE I hardly know where to
begin.

I had thought that salvation was God's ulti-
mate goal for me—that once I was saved and was
going to heaven, I had met that goal. I could not
have been more wrong. I had nothing to do with
my salvation except to accept the free, merciful gift
of spending eternity in the presence and fellowship
with Almighty God. *God did not want to be an*

event in my life; He wanted an ongoing, growing, intimate relationship with me: a thought that still blows my mind.

Not only that, while Jesus's saving me was paramount, it was only the tip of the iceberg. There was so much more that I had missed out on because of my pride, selfishness, and ignorance. And with that, I realized that while making a decision to receive Jesus was an integral part of the process, it by itself did not save me. I was saved because of the death of Jesus Christ on the cross. *Ephesians 2:8-9* makes it very clear:

"For it is by grace you have been saved, through faith—and this is not from yourselves, it is the gift of God—not by works, so that no one can boast."

I started to really grasp the tremendous price my salvation had required of Jesus. While it was free to me, it cost my Savior everything in order to reconcile me to God. *I Peter 1:18-19* is a constant reminder:

"For you know that it was not with perishable things such as silver or gold that you were redeemed from the empty way of life handed down to you from your ancestors, but with the precious blood of Christ, a lamb without blemish or defect."

It was finally becoming undeniable that Jesus needed to be more than my Savior, He required that He be *Lord* of my life. *He alone deserved to be my reason, my focus, my life, my everything.* I knew that I had a long way to go to make that a reality in my life, but for the first time, I longed for it to happen.

John 15:5 is an example of what a relationship with Jesus as Lord looks like:

"I am the vine, you are the branches. If a man remains in Me and I in him, he will bear much fruit; apart from Me, you can do nothing."

Yes, I had to take, once and for all, the first steps necessary to make that happen, and I wanted to remove the doubt that so often plagued me concerning my salvation. I got down on my knees, confessed and repented from my lazy Christianity, and asked Jesus into my heart, but this time not only as my Savior but also as my Lord (which was the missing part of my prayer from years before).

As amazing as it sounds, I finally learned that God's forgiveness, because of Jesus's death at Calvary, was complete. All my sins, *not some of my sins— sometimes, but all my sin, at all times*, had been forgiven. Not only that, I had been forever freed from sin, shame, and guilt—if I was willing to let go.

The Bible says in *Colossians 2:13-14*:

"When you were dead in your sins and in the uncircumcision of your flesh, God made you alive with Christ. He forgave us all our sins, having canceled the written code, with its regulations, that was against us and that stood opposed to us; which stood against us and condemned us; He took it away, nailing it to the cross."

The next stage was to not forget that baptism is an important, necessary, and commanded step in my relationship with God. *Romans 6:4* says:

"We were therefore buried with Him through baptism into death in order that, just as Christ was raised from the dead through the glory of the Father, we too may live a new life."

Baptism is one's *public declaration* to all, including Satan and his evil forces, that now as a child of God, I desire to be identified with Christ in His death and resurrection. I remembered that it was only after Jesus was baptized by John the Baptist and empowered by the Holy Spirit that His ministry started. If it was necessary for Jesus Christ to be empowered by the Holy Spirit to complete His mission, it must be good enough for me, too.

I was finally getting the picture. God had not only saved me from death and damnation, He had brought me into life in Him, for all eternity.

He had a purpose for my life, and salvation was only the beginning. In *Ephesians 2:10* we are told:

"For we are God's workmanship, created in Christ Jesus to do good works, which God prepared in advance for us to do."

As incredible as all that sounded to me, *God wanted to use me to live a life that would glorify Him.* WOW! At the beginning of this chapter, I quoted a passage from *II Corinthians 5* that tells me that God has called me to be His "ambassador of reconciliation." I am a representative of God to His people and to the people of this world who don't know Him. That thought was both thrilling and terrifying to me at the same time. Now I understood what the Great Commission was.

The good news was that God did not leave me alone and powerless to live the life He called me to live. He sent the Holy Spirit to live in me and to work through me to accomplish His purposes in my life. But I still had so much to learn about the Holy Spirit.

One of the most important things that I learned about the Third Person of the Trinity is that without Him, I would never have realized the truth of who God is, the wonder of His love, what salvation through Jesus was really all about, and the life that He had in store for me, was not only for eternity, but for now.

I Corinthians 2:10-12:

"The Spirit searches all things, even the deep things of God. For who knows a person's thoughts except their own spirit within them? In the same way no one knows the thoughts of God except the Spirit of God. What we have received is not the spirit of the world, but the Spirit who is from God, so that we may understand what God has freely given us."

I knew, first in my head, that I had received the Holy Spirit when I accepted Jesus as my Savior, but I eventually figured out that there was more than just receiving Him. *There was another step—the step of actually yielding to His place in my life.*

I learned that the Holy Spirit was not only the presence of God in my life, He was my source of truth, knowledge, and wisdom. He was also my guide and my deposit guaranteeing my salvation. In short, He was and always will be, the One who fully equips me to live the life that God has called me to live—I welcomed Him with all my heart.

Another amazing thing that I finally realized is that God views me very differently than I often view myself. I always thought that God saw me as I saw myself, a hypocritical Christian who failed way too often to live up to His expectations. No wonder I was always questioning His love for me. But I now know that because of Jesus's death on the cross and His continuous intercession on my behalf, I am viewed from God's perspective. I am now seen as one He loves beyond comprehension, a love based on His heart, not on my behavior.

I also learned that nothing can separate me from His love. Not only that, He wants to lavish His love on me and He delights in me, as it says in *Zephaniah 3:17*:

"The Lord your God is with you, He is mighty to save. He will take great delight in you, He will quiet you with His love, He will rejoice over you with singing."

I am finally at a place that, even though I do not understand why He would love me so much, I believe it, because He said so . . . and God cannot lie!

I was beginning to feel something toward God deep in my heart, something that I should have felt before but never really had—Love and Gratitude!

Thank God that He didn't give up on me. In His love and grace, He waited patiently until I was ready to begin to let go of myself and turn to Him, and when I did, He was waiting with open arms.

Moving Toward Growth:

1. Discuss the question at the beginning of the chapter: Is being saved God's only goal for me, or is there something more that I am missing?

2. Is your relationship with God a series of spiritual events or a 24/7 lifestyle?

3. What does it mean that God not only saved me "from" something, but He also saved me "for" something?

4. Why are you here? What is your purpose? Has God left you alone to fulfill that purpose?

6

MY
SELF-DECEPTION
ABOUT TRUST

Since God has proven Himself to be completely trustworthy in all ways in my life, why is my trust still limited and conditional?

Proverbs 28:26:
"Those who trust in themselves are fools, but those who walk in wisdom are kept safe."

II Corinthians 1:20-21:
"For no matter how many promises God has made, they are 'Yes' in Christ. And so through Him the 'Amen' is spoken by us to the glory of God. Now it is God who makes both us and you stand firm in Christ."

BOTTOM LINE, THERE IS NOTHING, or no one, in all of creation more trustworthy than God. There is nothing, or no one, who has gone to greater lengths to prove their trustworthiness to His stubborn, fallen creation than God. *He has kept every promise He has ever made. He is trustworthy in all He is, all He says, and in all He does.*

I knew enough by then that the Bible commanded me multiple times to "trust in the Lord." For example, when Jesus in *John 14:1* tells His disciples:

"Do not let your hearts be troubled. Trust in God; trust also in Me."

So, what was my problem with trusting God completely? It should be the simplest thing in the world to do, it was still so often hard. It was and is hard because I kept getting in the way. I have often said that, *"I would be a wonderful Christian if it wasn't for me."*

I found it difficult to trust for a couple of reasons:

First of all, I am not always trustworthy myself (and neither are the people around me). We, as people, have a great capacity for hurting each other. I like to think that most of the time we don't intend to, but it happens a lot. Some of the biggest ways we hurt each other are through dishonesty, disloyalty, and broken promises. We, as people, are simply not trustworthy by nature. The problem for me (and I believe for many others), is that *I was taking my human experience of lack of trust and applying it to my relationship with God.* My logic went something like this: Man is untrustworthy, and God created man; therefore, God is untrustworthy. I didn't say it was good logic; it was simply the way my developing Christian mind processed it. I needed to learn that, while my experience with people is flawed, my experiences of and with God have always been completely trustworthy, even if I didn't always understand His timing. That is a big lesson that I am still learning

The second barrier to my trust of God was born out of my own experiences in which I deemed God untrustworthy. I think back to the time when my five-year-old niece developed cancer. I remember how hard I (and the rest of the family) prayed for her healing, but my niece died anyway. It wasn't fair. We had prayed honorably, so how come God didn't give us the answer we wanted? When we wanted? How we wanted? Just an example of how I still had God on the performance-based acceptance program.

That is just one example of what God did that seemed to me to be untrustworthy. You see, I had God in a box, and whenever He stepped outside that box, my trust was broken. So, I had trusted God in some areas, and I kept what control I could in the others.

As in all the areas discussed so far in this book, I knew that I had a lot to learn, so I continued on that path, asking for wisdom and revelation as I moved along. *Isaiah 55:8-9* states it very clearly that there are times when I will not understand what God does.

"For My thoughts are not your thoughts, neither are your ways My ways," declares the Lord.

"As the heavens are higher than the earth, so are My ways higher than your ways and My thoughts than your thoughts."

I have a choice at those times: to trust God or not. I have to decide whether what the Bible says about God is true or not. If I believe that it is (which I do), then I have no reason to mistrust God. I just have to keep *myself* and *my feelings* out of His way. He has promised that He will always be with me, that He will walk with me through my entire life, and that He will see me through every circumstance that comes my way.

The question that I have to continually deal with is this: "Can I let God be God and still trust Him? YES!"

There are always going to be things happening in the world and in my life that I don't understand—hings that don't make sense to my way of thinking or timing. But God has an eternal plan that He is working out in everyone and all things for His glory. *He has every detail covered. He is God Almighty, after all.*

Not only that, He has given me the privilege of being part of that plan. I don't have to understand it; I just need to trust Him in it.

I still have a long way to go on my journey, but I am learning to trust Him more and more all the time—because He really is an amazing, faithful God!

The thought occurred to me recently that maybe the issue is not only can I trust God, but equally as important, can God trust me? He has entrusted me with His Word; He has made me an ambassador of reconciliation. Have I proven to be trustworthy with that calling, or has my lukewarm-ness caused me to be neglectful of the privilege with which God has entrusted me?

Moving Toward Growth:

1. Discuss the question at the beginning of the chapter: Since God has proven Himself to be completely trustworthy in all ways in my life, why is my trust still limited and conditional?

2. Has God ever done anything in my life that has caused me to lose trust in Him?

3. Why should I trust God?

4. Has lack of trust in God contributed to my lack of desire to grow?

5. In what ways does God show that He trusts me?

EPILOGUE

I almost missed it all!

I Corinthians 3:10-15:
"By the grace God has given me, I laid a foundation as wise builder, and someone else is building on it. But each one should build with care. For no one can lay any foundation other than the one already laid, which is Jesus Christ. If anyone builds on this foundation using gold, silver, costly stones, wood, hay, or straw, their work will be shown for what it is, because the Day will bring it to light. It will be revealed with fire, and the fire will test the quality of each person's work. If what has been built survives, the builder will receive a reward. If it is burned up, the builder will suffer loss but yet will be saved—even though only as one escaping through the flames."

So, WHAT NOW? I KNOW that there is more ahead for me than there is behind; maybe not in years on this earth, but certainly in my intimate fellowship with my Father in Heaven. I know that I can never be satisfied or complacent again with where I am in my walk with the Lord. But I also know that if I am not diligent, I can still slip back into my *saved and satisfied* life. I need to remember always that His design is a constant upward growth path, and He wants to guide me every step of the way through the Holy Spirit. But before I share with you about what this all means for me personally, I want to address something that concerns me greatly: My heart aches for anyone in the church who is where I was at the start of my journey—I have been calling it *saved and satisfied*.

I have three reasons for my deep concern:

1. The Bible makes it clear that a truly saved life shows fruit as evidence of the reality of salvation. I am not claiming to know which "fruit," or how much "fruit," I just know that the Word says in places such as *John 15:1-2* that the lack of fruit leads to being cut off from God:

"I am the True Vine and my Father is the gardener. He cuts off every branch in me that bears no fruit, while every branch that does bear fruit He prunes so it will be even more fruitful."

God is the only one who truly knows whose confessions are real and whose are false. I just know from experience that *saved and satisfied* is a tenuous place to be.

2. I ache, knowing personally what all of you are missing in that condition. I know that you seem

to be OK with where you are, and I know that you don't think you are missing anything, but obviously I've been there and I hope that from reading this book about my personal experience with the *saved and satisfied* mentality, you will begin to see all the wondrous things God has available for those who give themselves to Him as an instrument for His glory. (And I only scratched the surface.)

3. I am concerned for the church and the body of Christ as a whole. I have come to deeply love the church of God; not a particular building or denomination, but the people who make up the body. I would consider it a privilege beyond measure to be an instrument of encouragement and jump-start those believers who desire more of God and less of themselves to help the church become all God intended it to be in the world today. In order for the body of Christ to be totally effective, every member has to do his or her part. When so many in the church are content with just showing up, or wanting to be entertained, the church as a whole can never reach the maturity in Christ that God desires and commands.

I encourage you as brothers and sisters in Christ to step out in faith and *trust in God in all things* so we can begin to receive from God, through the power of the Holy Spirit, all that He wants to give us as we live our lives for Him and His glory.

Now, back to my personal lessons learned.

As mentioned earlier, I learned that salvation is

more about *bringing me into* something than it is about *saving me from* something. The Bible talks about being brought from death to life. I have learned that my new life is much more about God and others than it is about me: I have come to realize that while God has more to give than I will ever be able to receive, I want to receive all that I can, knowing now that God gives to me so I, in turn, can give to others.

I now have a fuller story to tell: a story of the wonder of God's grace and the forgiveness of sins through the shed blood of Jesus, with a new life of relationship with God empowered by the Holy Spirit. I always had a story, but I just didn't realize it. *Now, what I thought I couldn't tell, I can't wait to tell.*

We live in a scary, uncertain world. I, as an ambassador of God, have been called to do what I can to bring:

Love where there is hate.

Peace where there is conflict.

Comfort where there is pain.

Hope where there is despair.

Truth where there is deception.

Rest where there is stress.

Presence where there is loneliness.

Joy where there is sorrow.

Mercy where there is judgment.

Justice where there is injustice.

The wonder of God's grace, forgiveness, and love everywhere, to everyone God brings into my life.

Obviously, I am not responsible for doing this for every person in the world, but I am called to do so for those in my sphere of influence. This also must be done with prayer, wisdom, and discernment through the guidance of the Holy Spirit and knowledge of the Word of God. I am so blessed!

I hope to always be learning more about God, His Word, and His plan for my life. I pray that the wonder of His grace and the amazing sacrifice of Jesus on the cross will never be diminished in my life, because I didn't get out of the way or because life got too demanding. I want every day to be a new adventure in the Holy Spirit and to aspire every day to give more and more of myself to Him. I pray that someday, *Psalm 119:74* might be said of me:

"May those who fear You rejoice when they see me, for I have put my hope in your Word."

And that, ultimately, I will get to experience *Jude 1:24-25*:

"To Him Who is able to keep you from falling and to present you before His glorious presence without fault and with great joy—to the only God our Savior be glory, majesty, power, and authority, through Jesus Christ our Lord, before all ages now and forever more! Amen.

By the authority of Jesus Christ, the equipping of the Holy Spirit, and the power of God that raised Jesus from the dead, His promise to bring me home will be fulfilled. *And I no longer am satisfied with just getting into heaven smelling like smoke—*I want to hear the words of Jesus spoken in *Matthew 25:21*:

"Well done you good and faithful servant! You have been faithful with a few things; I will put you in charge of many things. Come and share your Master's happiness."

And all the praise be to God!

Moving Toward Growth:

1. What are you going to do about what you have learned?

2. Are you willing to let go of your saved and satisfied life, and exchange it for the life of growth God intends for you?

3. Are you willing to let go of more of yourself so you can experience true intimacy with God?

4. Will you live a life of complete trust in God and His promises so that, by the power of the Holy Spirit, other Christians can see what a life dedicated to the glory of God looks like?

"Now may the God of peace, who through the blood of the eternal covenant brought back from the dead our Lord Jesus, that great Shepherd of the sheep, equip you with everything good for doing His will, and may He work in us what is pleasing to Him, through Jesus Christ, to whom be glory forever and ever. Amen."
And Amen.
— *Hebrews 13:20-21*

ABOUT
THE AUTHOR

Dick Bont has been a pastor and counselor for the last twenty-five years. Through his teaching and writing, he has impacted thousands of lives for Christ. Though he has recently retired from church-affiliated active ministry, his desire to see people grow in Christ has not wavered. He continues to teach and counsel but spends most of his time writing books. *Confessions of a Lukewarm Christian* is Dick's third book, following *Life as It Should Be* and *What You Can't Earn*. Dick and his wife of thirty-plus years, Beth, reside in Ada, Michigan. Dick can be reached through his email, dbont49@gmail.com.

Made in the USA
Monee, IL
07 July 2020